For the Evetts

SALAD DAYS

Edited & Compiled by
Ursel Norman

Illustrated by
Derek Norman

WALDORF SALAD

Bon Appétit

SALAD DAYS

A collection of European and American salad recipes
compiled and edited by Ursel Norman
Illustrated by Derek Norman

Collins
Glasgow and London

First published 1975

Published by William Collins Sons & Company, Limited,
Glasgow & London

Printed in Great Britain

ISBN 0 00 435176 2

CONTENTS

INTRODUCTION

The Salad! A bowl of luscious, fresh greens coated with a smooth, subtle dressing, or raw vegetables, marinated and flavoured with a hint of spice or herbs. Such are the mouth-watering delights which can accompany the gourmet meal or family fare alike.

Why then is the salad so neglected, or even absent from the British dinner table? For the British, the salad is usually symbolized by the presence of a few wet lettuce leaves, a slice or two of tomato, some cucumber and a dash of salad cream.

This concept is enough to make many a continental cook cringe. For the continental European, the salad in one form or another is a source of infinite variety, always crisp and fresh, winter and summer alike. It is not as though there is any greater choice or supply of fresh vegetables, simply that the continental palate demands that a salad should give further colour and imagination to a meal, and complement and enhance the taste. Nor do they cling to a basic green salad, but frequently make use of seasonal vegetables.

Salad Days is an attempt to provide a collection of recipes and ideas which will stimulate the reader to discover the delights of the salad – a delight to the eye as well as the palate. Also, for those people who are already salad devotees, I hope the variety, and especially the inclusion of many less-familiar European salads, will give them renewed interest. I have tried to gather together a greater variety of recipes than is usually found in any one cookbook.

A good salad does not just happen, a lot of love and attention has to go into its preparation. Handle it gently at all times, and you will be rewarded by utmost crispness. The actual tossing of the finally assembled ingredients is, for most people, quite a ritual – something usually done at the dinner table, with infinite care being taken not to bruise a single leaf.

Creating a salad is truly underrated, for it can be a source of great joy. The pure tenderness of fresh greens serves to stimulate and refresh the palate, so that what accompanies or follows can be more fully appreciated. Nothing can match natural foods eaten when they are at their best, and most nutritious. Typical are the very humble, yet versatile Green Salad – a classic recipe – or Chef's Salad from America. In fact all the salads in the book are classics of one kind or another, all from different parts of the world, all with their own individual tastes and characteristics.

I have given emphasis to the use and suitability of certain vegetables at certain times of the year. Seasonal vegetables are at their best and cheapest when fresh. This is an added bonus, but by no means a prerequisite to the preparation of a fine salad.

The format of the book is designed for ease of use and understanding, so that the reader has an immediate indication of what the finished dish looks like. The visual step-by-step instructions convey the ease with which they can be made, while the introduction to each recipe gives a clue to the kind of taste to expect and with what they are best served.

Finally, whatever your motivation for discovering the salad, or rediscovering it, I trust that it will add colour, imagination and enjoyment to your cooking and eating. For that is what the delights of the salad are all about.

Bon appétit!

Ursel Norman

Derek Norman

Chicago 1974

7

HINTS ON HOW TO MAKE YOUR SALAD A HIT

THE DO'S & DON'TS

Here are some hints on the selection of ingredients and their preparation, which will help you to get the most out of your salad.

Lettuce
Handle it gently at all times! I have been horrified only too often to see a greengrocer stuff a lettuce into too small a paper bag, causing it to bruise. Bruises are waste – especially with Round and Cos lettuce, which are especially fragile. Webb and Curly Endive are less so.

Always wash the lettuce well, but make sure it is completely dry before tossing it with vinaigrette dressing because the dressing will not adhere to wet leaves. The best way to do this is to wrap the washed leaves in a towel (or paper towel) and leave them in the refrigerator for 2–3 hours. The towel helps to soak up the water, and the salad will

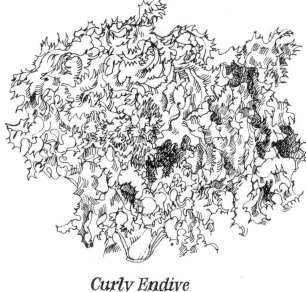

Webb

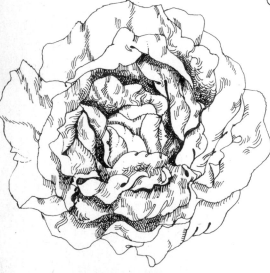

Round Lettuce

Cos

Curly Endive

The four most popular lettuces in Britain

8

come out crisp and dry. The dark in the refrigerator also helps because light tends to make lettuce leaves wilt more quickly.

Another way to dry lettuce is to shake the washed leaves gently in a wire basket or a colander, but take care not to bruise them.

Never cut lettuce with a knife, always tear it into bite-sized pieces. This gives the leaves a greater absorbency along the tear.

It is best not to toss the salad until just before serving – preferably at the dinner table – because it will go limp quite quickly once it comes into contact with the oil. However, I must admit that I cheat sometimes, when I have a lot of last-minute cooking to do. I make up the dressing in a bowl, pile the dried lettuce leaves loosely on top, and leave it in the refrigerator, covered with a paper towel, for an hour or even longer. Then all I need to do is toss it immediately before serving.

Cucumber

Cucumbers are often bitter at the blossom end. To avoid pulling the bitterness all through the cucumber, make it a habit to cut the cucumber in half first – and peel it from the cut edge to within 13 mm ($\frac{1}{2}$ inch) of the ends. Another point is that cucumbers shed a lot of water when they come into contact with salt, therefore it is advisable to sprinkle the peeled, sliced cucumber with some salt, and leave the slices to drain for at least half an hour in a colander. Then rinse off the salt, making sure the slices are quite dry before mixing them with the dressing.

Garlic

Some people find the use of garlic objectionable, therefore it is listed in most recipes as being optional. When it is not listed as being optional I would suggest that you should use it, for in such cases it is the only way to catch the authentic flavour of these salads.

Ask yourself why it is that you do not like it. Could it be that the smell of garlic follows you around – on your chopping board, your chopping knife, your fingers? If so, try sprinkling some salt on your chopping board, then dip your knife into it. Then cut or crush your garlic clove in the salt. You will not smell a thing!

Sometimes it is enough just to rub a salad bowl with a cut clove of garlic; this way you do not actually eat it. Another way to give a salad a slight garlic flavour is the French way of rubbing a piece of stale bread with a cut clove of garlic and then tossing it around with the greens and the dressing. Remove the bread before serving the salad. This piece of bread is known as a *chapon*.

Oil

Most cookbooks will have you believe that only olive oil will do. Authentic vinaigrette dressing does indeed call for olive oil, but in fact any oil found on your supermarket shelf can be used. You might even prefer it to olive oil, which is very heavy. Only in recipes where I specifically recommend olive oil would I urge you to use it for maximum authenticity.

Vinegar

The same applies to vinegar. Red or white wine vinegars are undoubtedly more delicious, but try buying the unflavoured ones. Then you can add your own flavourings, either herbs from your garden or dried ones from your kitchen shelf. This brings more variety into your dressings. Ordinary vinegars are also most enjoyable though, and certainly much cheaper, and added herbs give them quite a unique flavour. You will find that I have mostly used ordinary vinegars in my recipes.

Instead of vinegar you can use an equal quantity of fresh lemon juice. This can make a very pleasant change. If the lemon dressing seems a little sour, add a sprinkle of sugar to it.

Salad Bowls

The ideal salad bowl for tossed salads is a large wooden one, with a large wooden spoon and fork. The softness of the wood is least likely to bruise the salad. They should be washed quickly (never soaked) in warm soapy water and dried straight away.

Glass bowls are also very attractive, as are china or ceramic ones. Just make sure they are not made of a porous material, in other words, they must be well glazed. Naturally you would not let vinegar touch silver or metal bowls.

Salad Dressings

For tossed green or mixed salads only a vinaigrette dressing (oil, vinegar or lemon) is acceptable. I tend to have a personal dislike for all the creamy concoctions in bottles and jars. I find home-made ones acceptable, though only on Webb lettuce, since this is the only kind of lettuce that does not collapse under a heavy dressing. A salad is designed to stimulate the palate, but a salad with a creamy dressing tends to have the reverse effect. However, for those who cannot live without creamy dressings I have given recipes for some of the more popular ones on page 64.

As regards mayonnaise, I would like to stress that you should only use a good commercial one, or, better still, make your own. The recipe is on page 64.

Never, never use any kind of commercial salad cream for any of the recipes in this book.

When and How to Serve

Salads can start a meal and be served as an hors d'oeuvre, or go with a meal and accompany the main dish, or come after the main course. When eaten before a meal as an hors d'oeuvre, the salad should be served on individual chilled plates, and eaten with just a fork. The same applies to salads eaten after the main course. Salads eaten with the main course are best served on individual plates or small bowls and placed at the top left hand side of the dinner plate. It is also quite acceptable to serve a salad on the same plate as the main course, especially with rice or pasta dishes, when no vegetable is served.

One note of advice: always serve a salad at some point during a dinner party. Your guests will appreciate the fresh, cool change.

Diet conscious or not, a salad can make an ideal meal in itself.

Winter Salads

In the depths of winter, resort to hothouse lettuces, red and green cabbages, Dutch cabbage, potatoes, the occasional cucumber or tomato, and tinned stuffs, such as green beans, or asparagus. Fresh mushrooms are usually available even in mid-winter.

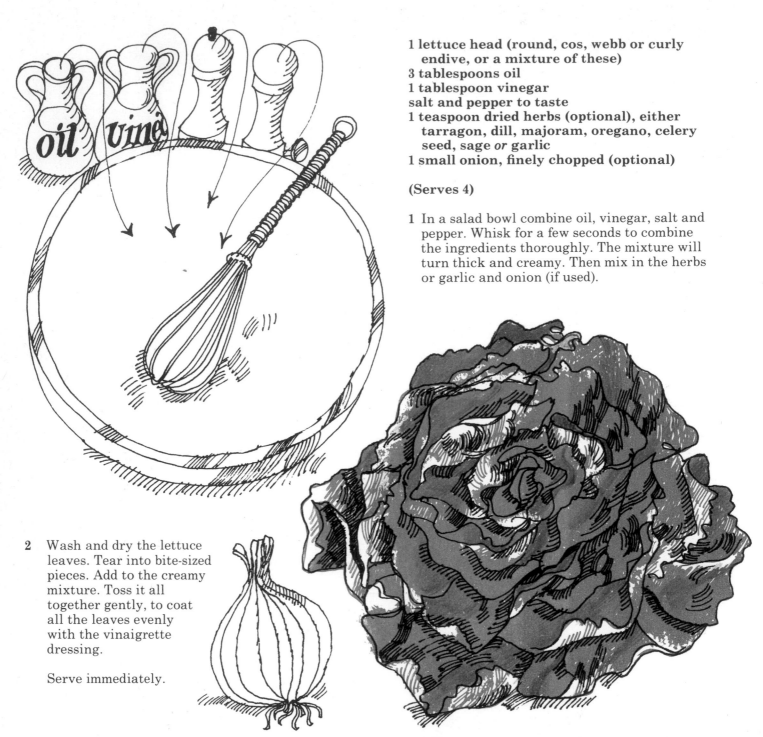

1 lettuce head (round, cos, webb or curly
   endive, or a mixture of these)
3 tablespoons oil
1 tablespoon vinegar
salt and pepper to taste
1 teaspoon dried herbs (optional), either
   tarragon, dill, majoram, oregano, celery
   seed, sage *or* garlic
1 small onion, finely chopped (optional)

(Serves 4)

1 In a salad bowl combine oil, vinegar, salt and
   pepper. Whisk for a few seconds to combine
   the ingredients thoroughly. The mixture will
   turn thick and creamy. Then mix in the herbs
   or garlic and onion (if used).

2 Wash and dry the lettuce
   leaves. Tear into bite-sized
   pieces. Add to the creamy
   mixture. Toss it all
   together gently, to coat
   all the leaves evenly
   with the vinaigrette
   dressing.

   Serve immediately.

Note:
The Green Salad is also the basis for making a
Mixed Salad – simply add your own choice of
vegetables (tomato, cucumber, radishes,
watercress, mustard cress, red and green peppers,
sliced mushrooms, etc.).

The Basic Green Salad

This is probably the world's most popular and versatile salad. The classic French vinaigrette dressing gives it a tangy kind of flavour, guaranteed to refresh the palate. As a side dish the green salad will accompany any main course. It is a must with all rice and pasta dishes.

When you are unsure which vegetable to have with a certain dish, the green salad will always prove an excellent choice.

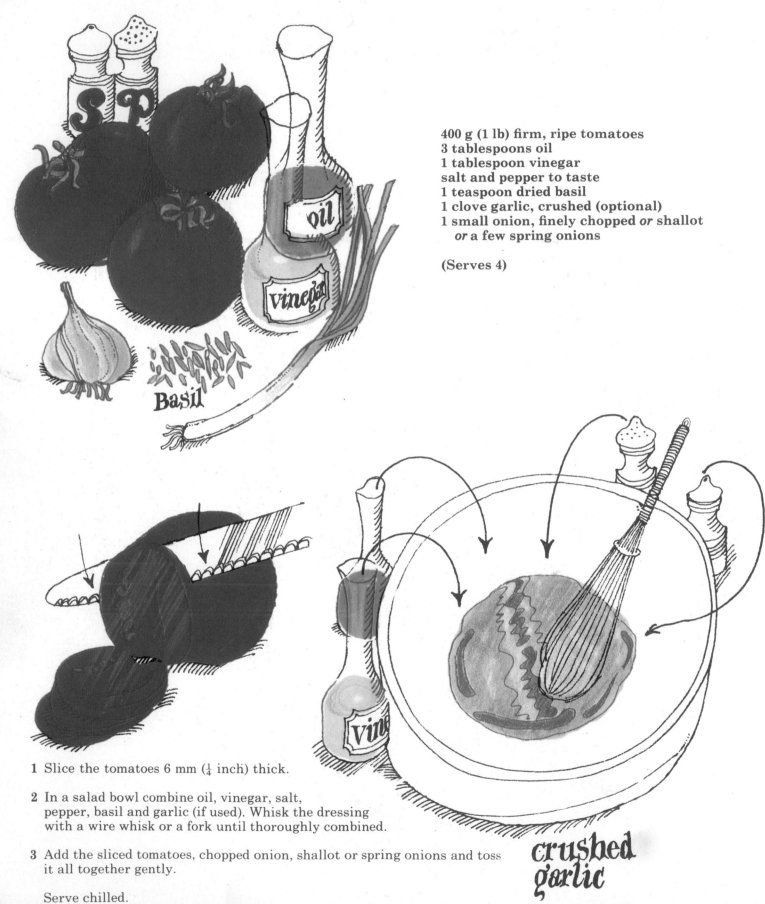

400 g (1 lb) firm, ripe tomatoes
3 tablespoons oil
1 tablespoon vinegar
salt and pepper to taste
1 teaspoon dried basil
1 clove garlic, crushed (optional)
1 small onion, finely chopped *or* shallot
   or a few spring onions

(Serves 4)

Basil

1 Slice the tomatoes 6 mm ($\frac{1}{4}$ inch) thick.

2 In a salad bowl combine oil, vinegar, salt,
pepper, basil and garlic (if used). Whisk the dressing
with a wire whisk or a fork until thoroughly combined.

3 Add the sliced tomatoes, chopped onion, shallot or spring onions and toss
it all together gently.

Serve chilled.

crushed
garlic

TOMATO SALAD

Especially fine in summer, when tomatoes are at their peak. Cool and
juicy, it is ideal for serving with fried dishes – particularly steak, chops or fish.
A bowl of tomato salad will add a brilliant splash of colour to the dinner table.
A touch of basil, together with the garlic, highlights the authentic
continental flavour of this recipe.

1 cucumber
2 tablespoons oil
2 tablespoons vinegar
salt and pepper to taste
$\frac{1}{4}$ teaspoon dried dill
3–4 spring onions, chopped *or* 1 small onion, chopped
1 tablespoon double cream *or* evaporated milk

(Serves 4)

1 Peel the cucumber (see page 9) and slice into very, very thin slices. Place them in a colander. Sprinkle a little salt over the slices and leave them to drain for 30 minutes. Rinse them with cold water and dry thoroughly with paper towels.

2 In a bowl whisk together the oil, vinegar, salt, pepper and dill. Mix in the spring onions and the cream.

3 Toss the cucumber slices in the bowl to coat them evenly with the dressing.

Serve chilled.

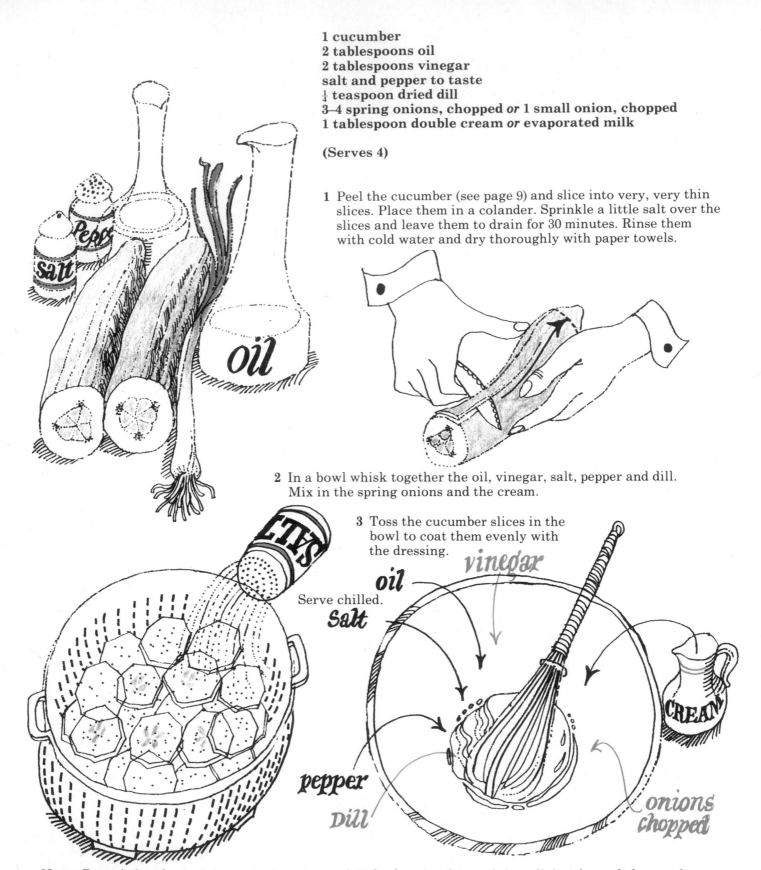

Note: By omitting the draining procedure (preparing the dressing first and then slicing the peeled cucumber into it) the dressing will be diluted by the juice from the cucumber. This also makes a delicious salad, and children love the juice.

CUCUMBER SALAD

This beautifully juicy salad with a taste of spring is very smooth on the palate, and is ideal with rice dishes or new, buttered potatoes. The addition of dill gives it a slightly sweet and very delicate taste. A favourite with children.

400 g (1 lb) good, small potatoes
(They must stay in one piece when
boiled, new ones are usually the safest.)
2 tablespoons vinegar
½ teaspoon sugar
salt and pepper to taste

1 small onion, finely chopped
1 heaped tablespoon chopped gherkin
(optional)
3–4 heaped tablespoons good mayonnaise
1 hard-boiled egg, cut into wedges
a little chopped parsley

(Serves 3 or 4)

1 Leave the skin on the potatoes, then boil them until tender
in salted water. Drain and leave them to cool.

2 Meanwhile, put the vinegar,
sugar, salt and pepper into a
bowl and whisk to combine.
Add chopped onion and gherkin
(if used) and the peeled,
thinly sliced potatoes.
(Halve the larger potatoes to keep
all the slices small.)

3 Add the mayonnaise, mix it all
well and garnish with the hard-
boiled egg and chopped parsley

4 Leave to marinate for 1 hour.

Note: This salad will keep
for a day or two if kept
tightly covered in a refrigerator. To freshen it up
again, toss in 1 tablespoon
of boiling water before
serving.

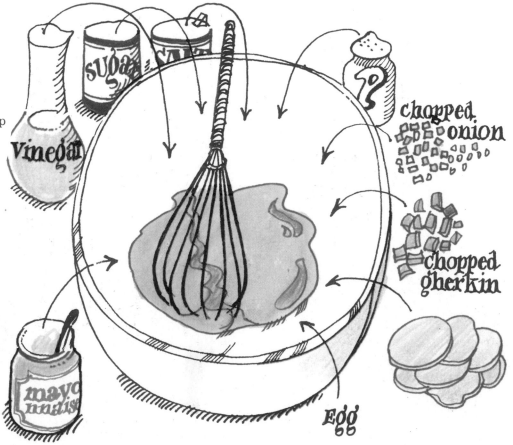

Kartoffel Salat

I always think of this salad as being distinctly German, and this is an authentic German recipe. The taste is especially fine with frankfurters, any cold meat, and, would you believe it, fried fish. You may find it even more to your liking than chips. In Germany no picnic is complete without the potato salad.

1 small Dutch cabbage, about 400 g (1 lb)
salt and pepper to taste
½ teaspoon sugar
2 tablespoons vinegar
1 small green pepper, deseeded and sliced (optional)
1 teaspoon celery seed (optional)
3 tablespoons good mayonnaise
chopped chives *or* parsley

(Serves 4–6)

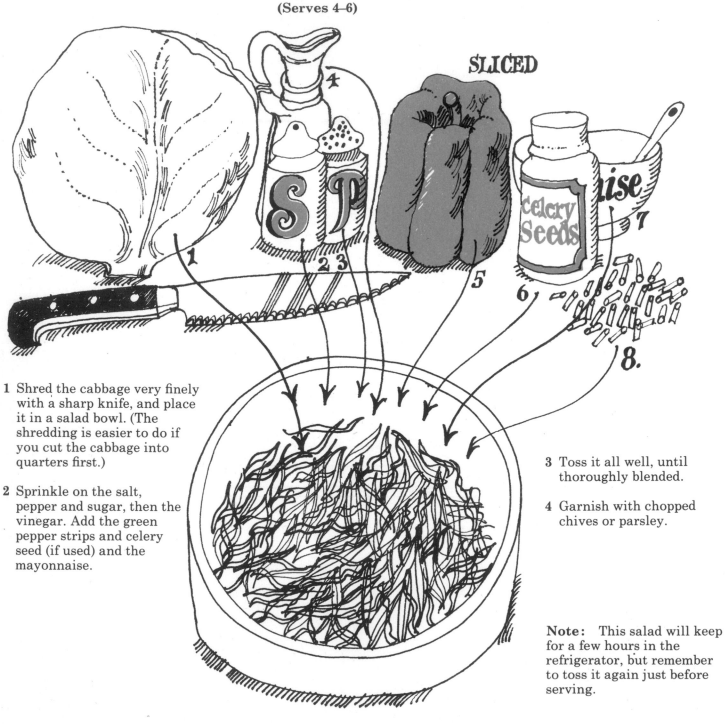

1 Shred the cabbage very finely with a sharp knife, and place it in a salad bowl. (The shredding is easier to do if you cut the cabbage into quarters first.)

2 Sprinkle on the salt, pepper and sugar, then the vinegar. Add the green pepper strips and celery seed (if used) and the mayonnaise.

3 Toss it all well, until thoroughly blended.

4 Garnish with chopped chives or parsley.

Note: This salad will keep for a few hours in the refrigerator, but remember to toss it again just before serving.

COLESLAW

Coleslaw is something I have
been eating as long as I can
remember. It is especially popular
on the Continent and in North America.
Its creamy dressing makes it ideal as an
accompaniment to fish, chips or hamburger, or
for that matter, any fried meat.

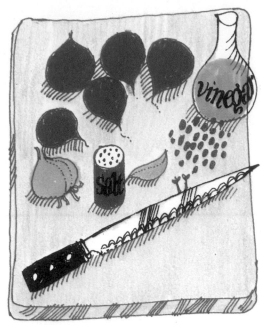

800 g (2 lbs) cooked beetroot, cut into slices
1 large onion, cut into rings
100 ml (4 fl oz) vinegar
100 ml (4 fl oz) water
1 dessertspoon sugar
1 bayleaf
4 peppercorns
2 whole cloves
½ teaspoon salt
½ teaspoon caraway seeds (optional)

(Serves 4)

1 Cook the beetroot in salted water until tender, peel them and cut them into slices.

2 Place them in a deep, china or glass dish together with the onion rings.

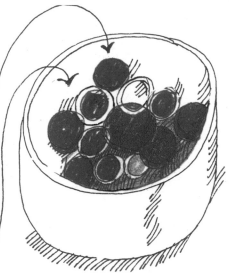

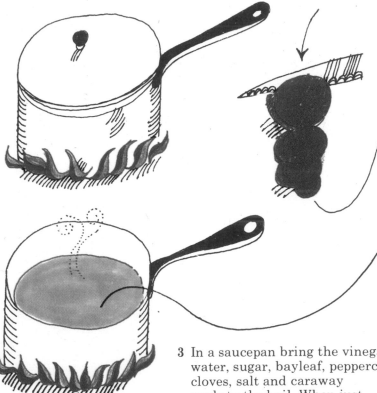

3 In a saucepan bring the vinegar, water, sugar, bayleaf, peppercorns, cloves, salt and caraway seeds to the boil. When just reaching boiling point, pour this marinade over the beetroot and onions.

4 Leave to cool and then refrigerate until ready to use.

Note: This salad will keep for about a week if tightly covered and kept in the refrigerator.

Beetroot Salad

This salad was one of my Grandmother's favourites. The marinade gives it a unique taste and distinctive, old-fashioned kind of flavour. Especially good with cold meats, fried fish and potato dishes. In Britain greengrocers often sell beetroot already boiled, which makes things much easier.

Especially good for weight watchers – almost zero calories.

400 g (1 lb) green string beans *or* 1 large tin cut green beans
3 tablespoons oil
1 tablespoon vinegar
salt and pepper to taste
1 small onion, finely chopped *or* shallot *or* some spring onions
½ teaspoon dried tarragon, oregano, dill or garlic (optional)
1 sprig of parsley for garnish

(Serves 4)

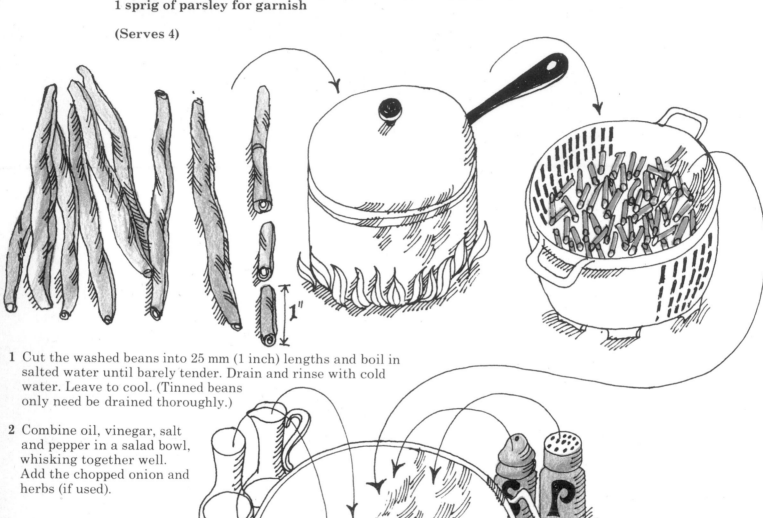

1 Cut the washed beans into 25 mm (1 inch) lengths and boil in
   salted water until barely tender. Drain and rinse with cold
   water. Leave to cool. (Tinned beans
   only need be drained thoroughly.)

2 Combine oil, vinegar, salt
   and pepper in a salad bowl,
   whisking together well.
   Add the chopped onion and
   herbs (if used).

3 Add the cooled beans and toss it
   all together gently. Leave to
   marinate for 1 hour in a cool
   place.

4 Toss again just before serving
   and garnish with parsley.

Bohnensalat

An old German salad. This is my own recipe,
inherited from my mother, who inherited it
from her mother, who I suspect inherited it
from her mother. However, this particular version
I like to feel is distinguished by its simplicity.
Smooth and soft, it can be served instead of a vegetable
with just about any dish.

4 firm green peppers
1 clove garlic
¼ teaspoon salt
5 tablespoons olive oil
1 small tin pimientos
   ***or* add 1 red pepper to the green ones**
a few stoned black olives

(Serves 4)

1 To skin the peppers spear them on a
   fork and scorch the skin over a flame
   until it turns quite black, then
   scrape it off with a knife.

2 Cut the skinned peppers into
   quarters and remove all the seeds.
   Then cut them into strips.

3 Crush the clove of garlic into the
   salt, until it turns almost to a
   liquid, then with a wire whisk beat
   in the oil in a thin, steady stream.

4 Arrange the peppers attractively on a
   platter, scatter the pimientos (or the red
   pepper strips) over them, and pour the
   dressing over. Garnish with the olives.
   Cover the dish and leave the flavours to
   mingle for 30–60 minutes.

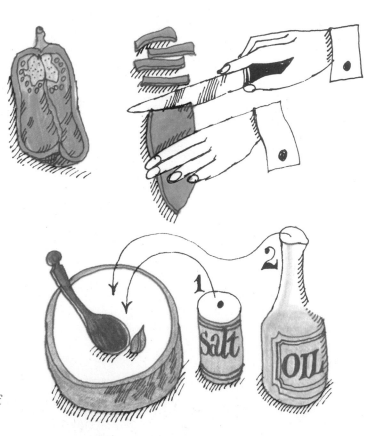

Note: This salad will keep for 2–3 days if
kept tightly covered in a refrigerator.

Green Pepper Salad Provençale

A truly magnificent French recipe – a mediterranean delight. The grace and flavour of this salad complements almost any meal, or alternatively it can be served as part of an hors d'oeuvre. You will find its taste smooth, soft and unusually different.

200 g (½ lb) firm, green or white cabbage, thinly shredded
200 g (½ lb) red cabbage, thinly shredded
salt and pepper to taste
1 green pepper, deseeded and cut into strips (optional)
1 small onion, thinly sliced
4 tablespoons oil
2 tablespoons vinegar
1 tablespoon chopped parsley

(Serves 4–6)

1 Cut both cabbages into quarters and shred them very thinly with a sharp knife. Discard the core.

2 Place the shredded cabbage in a bowl, add the salt, pepper, green pepper strips and onion rings. Toss lightly.

3 In a screwtop jar combine oil and vinegar and shake until thoroughly blended.

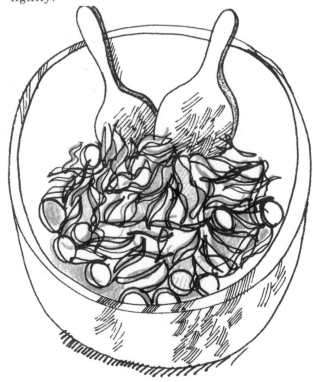

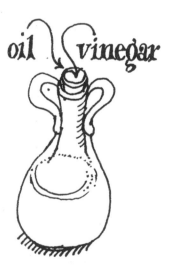

4 Pour it over the salad, toss it thoroughly and refrigerate until ready to use.

5 Just before serving toss it again lightly and sprinkle with the chopped parsley.

RAW CABBAGE SALAD

An extremely crunchy, tangy and crisp salad, which is highly nutritious, and can be eaten any time of the year. The cabbage salad has a certain earthiness which is always refreshing and stimulating to the palate. It makes a fine winter salad.

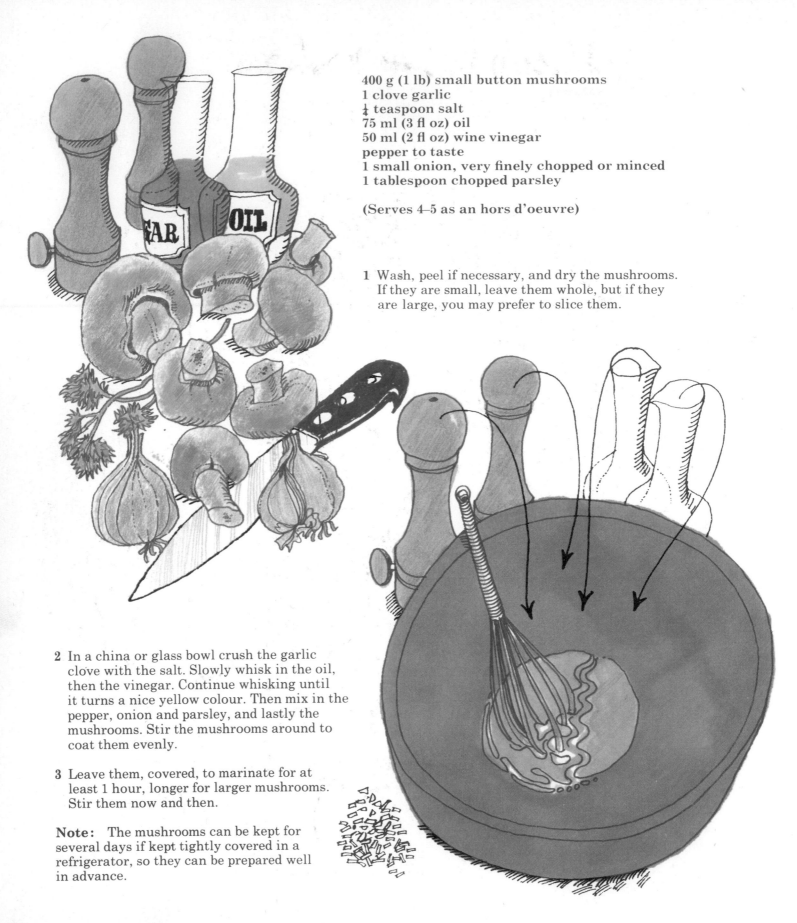

400 g (1 lb) small button mushrooms
1 clove garlic
¼ teaspoon salt
75 ml (3 fl oz) oil
50 ml (2 fl oz) wine vinegar
pepper to taste
1 small onion, very finely chopped or minced
1 tablespoon chopped parsley

(Serves 4–5 as an hors d'oeuvre)

1 Wash, peel if necessary, and dry the mushrooms.
   If they are small, leave them whole, but if they
   are large, you may prefer to slice them.

2 In a china or glass bowl crush the garlic
   clove with the salt. Slowly whisk in the oil,
   then the vinegar. Continue whisking until
   it turns a nice yellow colour. Then mix in the
   pepper, onion and parsley, and lastly the
   mushrooms. Stir the mushrooms around to
   coat them evenly.

3 Leave them, covered, to marinate for at
   least 1 hour, longer for larger mushrooms.
   Stir them now and then.

Note: The mushrooms can be kept for
several days if kept tightly covered in a
refrigerator, so they can be prepared well
in advance.

Mushroom Salad

A magnificent and unusual taste. The marinade 'cooks' the mushrooms to leave them soft and absolutely delicious. Mushroom salad can be served as an hors d'oeuvre, or as part of a buffet.

1 small celeriac
38 g (1½ oz) chopped walnuts
200 g (8 oz) green grapes, pips removed
1 small eating apple
juice of 1 lemon
4 tablespoons good mayonnaise
salt and pepper to taste
chives or parsley, chopped, for garnish

(Serves 4)

1 Boil the celeriac in salted water until tender; at least 30 minutes. Test as for potatoes.

2 Peel off the skin and cut into 13 mm (½-inch) cubes.

chopped walnuts.

Lemon Juice

deseeded grapes.

3 Place the cubes in a salad bowl. Add the roughly chopped walnuts and the deseeded grapes. Peel the apple and cut it into small pieces. Coat the apple pieces with lemon juice to prevent them discolouring. Add to the salad bowl.

4 Make up a dressing of the mayonnaise, leftover lemon juice, salt and pepper. Add the dressing to the salad and toss it all together lightly but thoroughly.

5 Refrigerate until ready to use, then sprinkle on the chives or parsley.

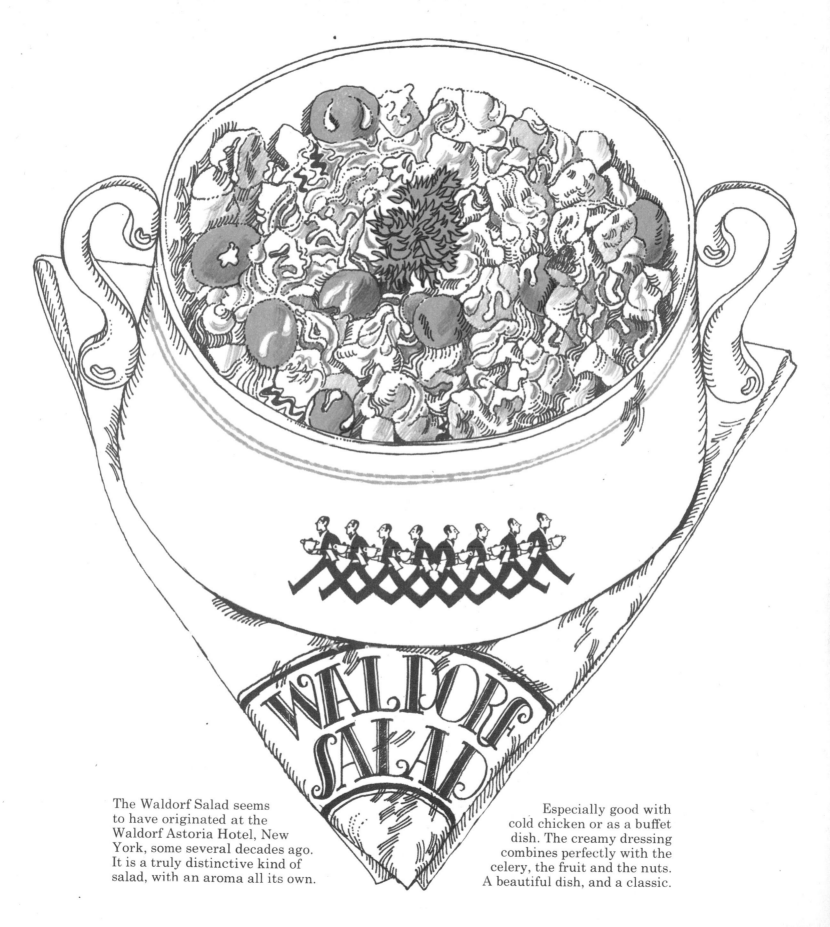

WALDORF SALAD

The Waldorf Salad seems to have originated at the Waldorf Astoria Hotel, New York, some several decades ago. It is a truly distinctive kind of salad, with an aroma all its own.

Especially good with cold chicken or as a buffet dish. The creamy dressing combines perfectly with the celery, the fruit and the nuts. A beautiful dish, and a classic.

2 lettuce hearts
2 tins tuna fish
10 or so stoned black olives
1 onion, cut into rings
2 tomatoes, cut into wedges
100 g (4 oz) or more cooked string beans
1 green pepper, cut into strips
1 hard-boiled egg, cut into wedges
100 ml (4 fl oz) olive oil
50 ml (2 fl oz) white wine vinegar
¼ teaspoon dried tarragon
¼ teaspoon dried dill
salt and pepper to taste
1 clove garlic, crushed

(Serves 4 for lunch or 6 as an hors d'oeuvre)

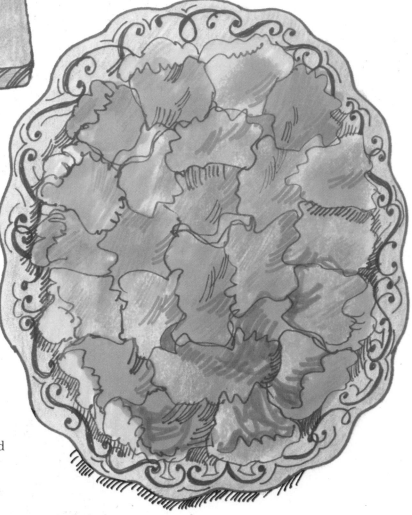

1 Wash and dry the lettuce and tear it into bite-sized pieces. Line a nice platter with it.

2 Mound the tuna fish in the centre and garnish the platter attractively with olives, onion rings, tomatoes, string beans, pepper strips and wedges of hard-boiled egg.

3 Make a vinaigrette dressing from the rest of the ingredients in a screwtop jar or bottle, and shake it to combine it all thoroughly.

4 Pour the dressing over the salad and serve immediately.

Note: Niçoise salad lends itself to great variations. Sometimes it can also include boiled and cubed potato, anchovy fillets, cooked artichoke bottoms or peas.

SALAD NIÇOISE

A French provincial classic, generally accepted as originating in Nice. A truly great salad, which is almost a complete meal in itself.

Its combination of ingredients give it a wholesome country character, ideal for a summer lunch. It can also be served as an hors d'oeuvre.

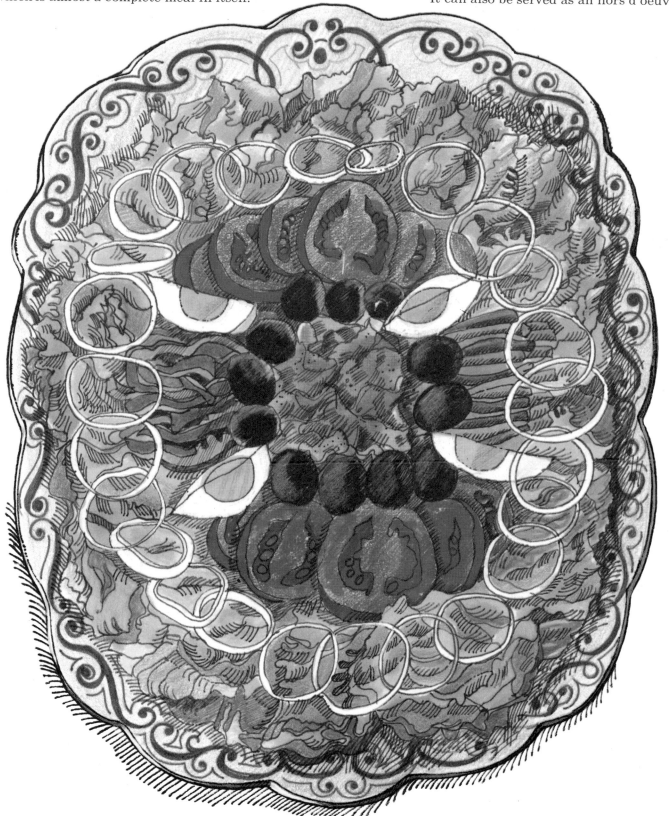

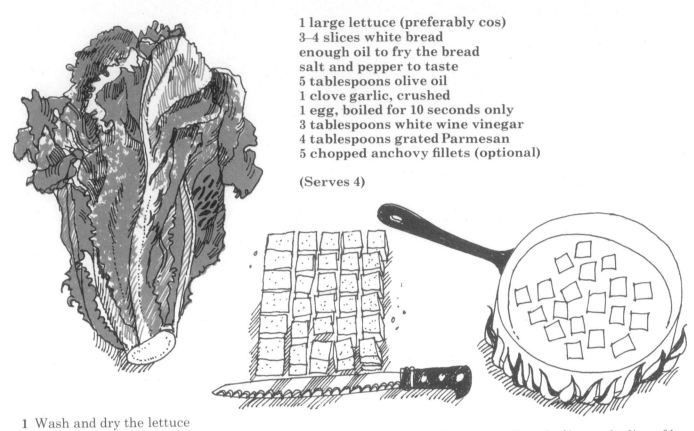

1 large lettuce (preferably cos)
3–4 slices white bread
enough oil to fry the bread
salt and pepper to taste
5 tablespoons olive oil
1 clove garlic, crushed
1 egg, boiled for 10 seconds only
3 tablespoons white wine vinegar
4 tablespoons grated Parmesan
5 chopped anchovy fillets (optional)

(Serves 4)

1 Wash and dry the lettuce well, wrap in a towel and refrigerate until ready to use.

2 To make *croutons*, cut the crusts off, and cube, each slice of bread. Fry the cubes in oil until nicely browned all round.

3 Now tear the lettuce into bite-sized pieces and put into a large salad bowl. Add the salt and pepper and the olive oil and crushed garlic and toss gently.

4 Break the egg over it, add the vinegar and toss again lightly.

5 Sprinkle the Parmesan and anchovy fillets (if used) over it all and toss again lightly.

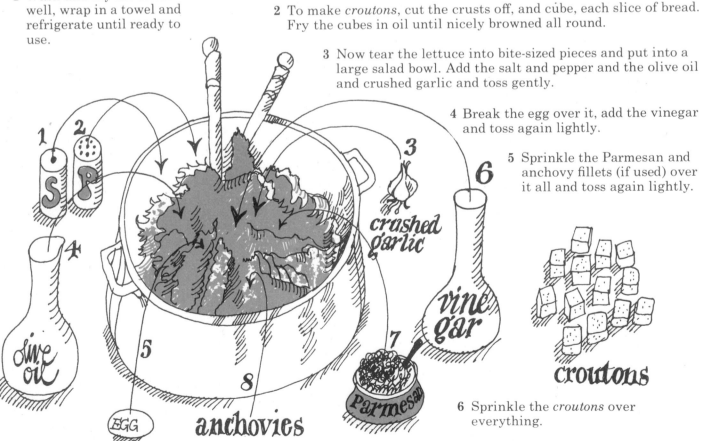

6 Sprinkle the *croutons* over everything.

Serve immediately.

Caesar Salad

A southern Californian classic. The rich tender greens make a particularly crisp salad. The fresh flavour of the dressing make it a highly distinctive dish for the connoisseur or novice alike. There are numerous variations of the Caesar Salad, but to the best of my knowledge this recipe is the most authentic.

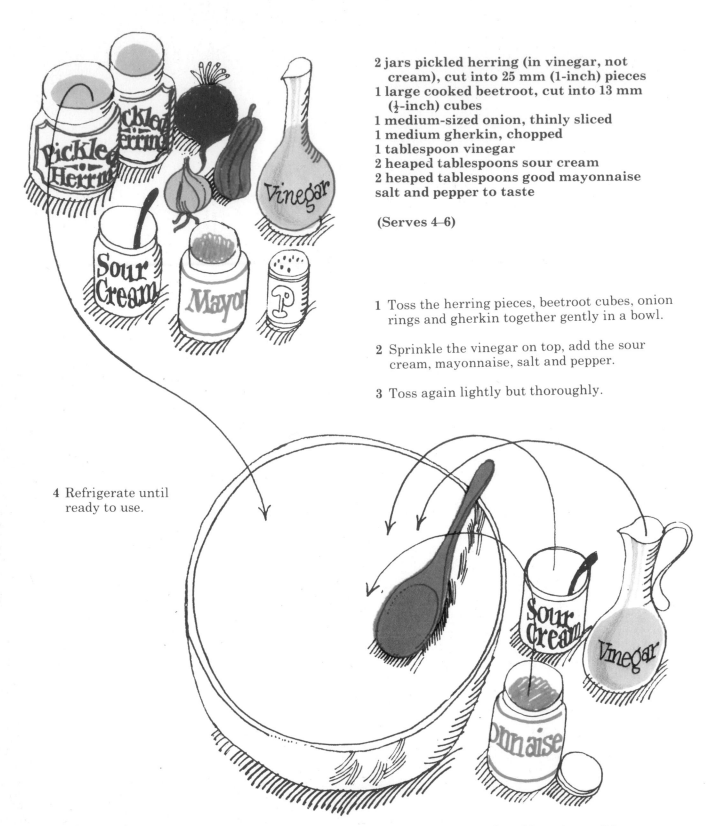

2 jars pickled herring (in vinegar, not cream), cut into 25 mm (1-inch) pieces
1 large cooked beetroot, cut into 13 mm (½-inch) cubes
1 medium-sized onion, thinly sliced
1 medium gherkin, chopped
1 tablespoon vinegar
2 heaped tablespoons sour cream
2 heaped tablespoons good mayonnaise
salt and pepper to taste

(Serves 4–6)

1 Toss the herring pieces, beetroot cubes, onion rings and gherkin together gently in a bowl.

2 Sprinkle the vinegar on top, add the sour cream, mayonnaise, salt and pepper.

3 Toss again lightly but thoroughly.

4 Refrigerate until ready to use.

Note: This salad will keep for a day or two if tightly covered and kept in a refrigerator.

Hering Salat

A simple version of an authentic German recipe. Creamy, fishy and beautifully smooth. It makes an ideal hors d'oeuvre or buffet dish, or, as a midnight snack after a late night out, it will help to clear your head the morning after.

1 onion, thinly sliced
1 orange, cut into segments
4 tablespoons oil
4 tablespoons vinegar
salt and pepper to taste
1 lettuce head

(Serves 4)

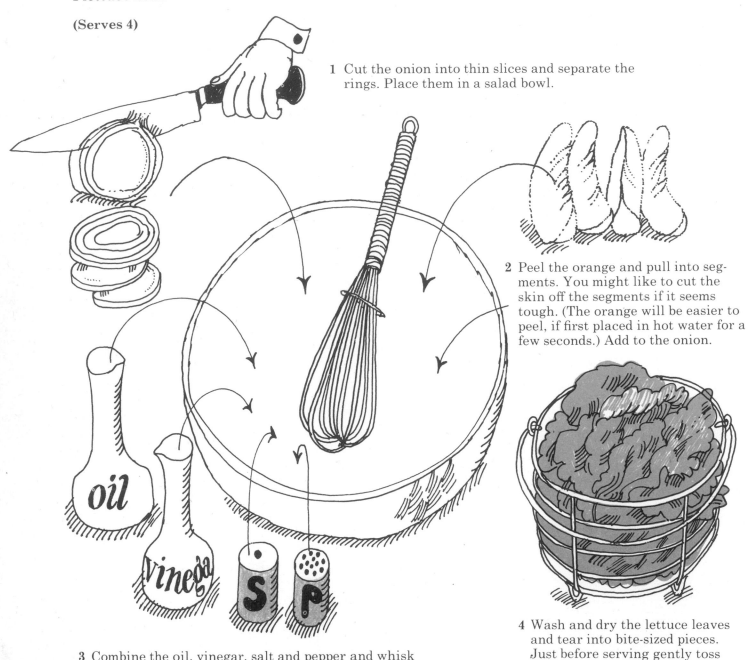

1 Cut the onion into thin slices and separate the rings. Place them in a salad bowl.

2 Peel the orange and pull into segments. You might like to cut the skin off the segments if it seems tough. (The orange will be easier to peel, if first placed in hot water for a few seconds.) Add to the onion.

3 Combine the oil, vinegar, salt and pepper and whisk until well blended. Pour this mixture over the onions and orange. Cover the bowl and leave to marinate in the refrigerator for 1 hour.

4 Wash and dry the lettuce leaves and tear into bite-sized pieces. Just before serving gently toss the lettuce in the marinade.

Serve immediately.

Spanish Salad

The orange and onion give this salad a really
delightful flavour. Crisp, juicy and truly
refreshing, it is a salad that can be enjoyed at
any time of the year.

The combination of flavours goes well with
light meat, chicken or fish.

1 lettuce head (preferably Webb)
200 g (8 oz) cold, cooked chicken, cubed
100 g (4 oz) thick sliced ham, cubed
100 g (4 oz) cheese, cubed (any kind)
2 hard-boiled eggs, cut into wedges
2 tomatoes, cut into wedges
1 bunch watercress
5 spring onions
a Salad Dressing from page 64 *or* the
  vinaigrette dressing for Salad Niçoise,
  pages 34–5

(Serves 4)

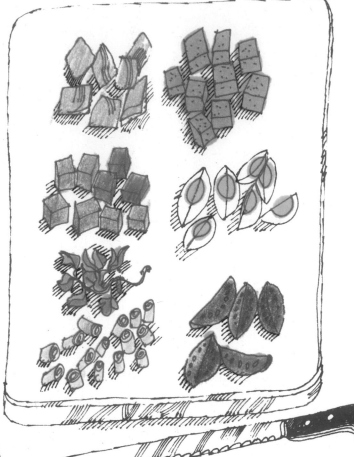

1 Wash and dry all the vegetables. Tear the lettuce into bite-sized pieces, and place in a wide, shallow bowl or on a platter.

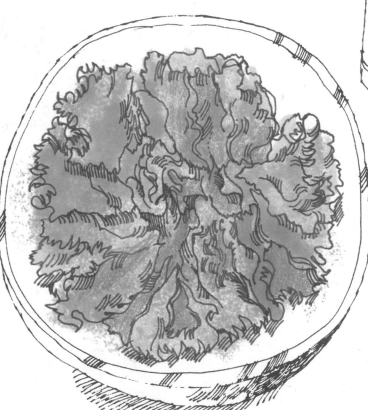

2 On top of the lettuce arrange the chicken cubes, ham cubes, cheese cubes, egg wedges, tomato wedges, watercress and spring onions, in an attractive pattern.

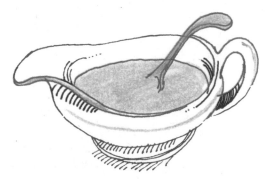

3 Pass the dressing separately in a small bowl. Let everyone help themselves to the salad first, and then pour the dressing over to suit their own taste.

Chef's Salad.

This is generally recognised as an American salad. It makes an ideal light lunch or supper and is refreshing on a hot summer's day. Try it with a glass of wine and a chunk of crusty bread, or as a picnic salad.

enough raw spinach for your needs
1 small cucumber
salt
2 tablespoons red wine vinegar
4 tablespoons oil
pepper to taste
a little dry mustard

(Serves 4)

1 Wash the spinach well and clean off any tough
leaves and stems. Leave to dry completely.

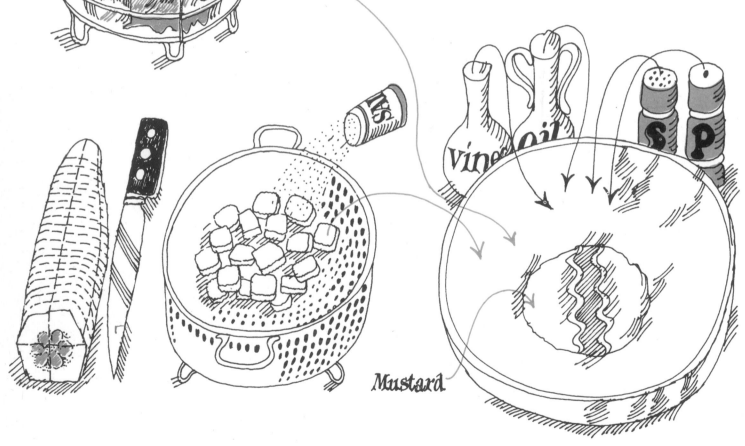

Mustard

2 Peel the cucumber and cut into small cubes and
place them in a colander. Sprinkle on some salt
and leave to drain for at least 30 minutes. Rinse
with cold water and leave to dry.

3 Mix the vinegar, oil, salt, pepper and dry
mustard together in a salad bowl, add the
spinach and the cucumber and toss together
gently but thoroughly.

Serve immediately.

A salad of good, earthy character, honest and sincere. The combination of spinach and velvety cucumber, plus the dressing, gives this salad a distinctive taste all its own. It is zesty, robust and highly nutritious.

It is the only way my children will eat spinach. It provides an unusual accompaniment to any main course.

200–300 g (8–12 oz) lean, cooked, cold meat
   (leftover veal, beef, pork or lamb, cut into
   julienne strips about 25 mm (1 inch) long
   and 6 mm (¼ inch) wide)
100 g (4 oz) green peas
1 large carrot, cooked and cubed
2 cold, boiled potatoes, cubed
2 gherkins, cubed
1 medium onion, cut into julienne strips
25 ml (1 fl oz) vinegar
3–4 tablespoons juice from gherkins
salt and pepper to taste
1 level teaspoon sugar
1 small carton sour cream
chopped parsley or chives for garnish

(Serves 4–6)

2 Make a marinade of vinegar, gherkin juice, salt and
pepper and the sugar and pour it over the salad in the
bowl.

1 Place all the meat and vegetables in a
salad bowl.

3 Leave to marinate in the refrigerator for an hour or
longer, tossing it once in a while.

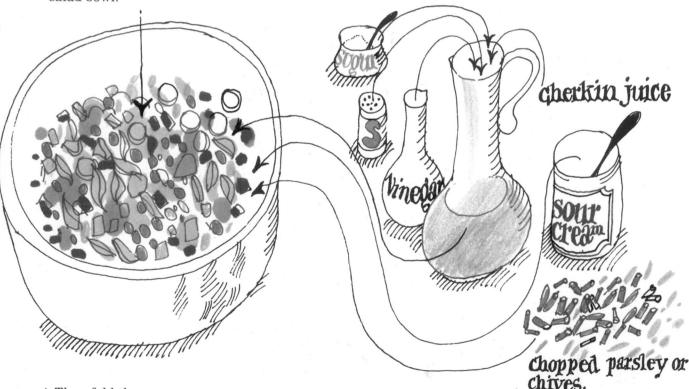

4 Then fold the sour cream
in gently but thoroughly

5 Dust with chopped parsley or
chives.

Note: This salad will keep for a day or two if tightly
covered and kept in a refrigerator.
  You can also use cooked green beans, broad beans, capers,
black or green olives, cooked beetroot or cooked mushrooms.

RUSSIAN SALAD

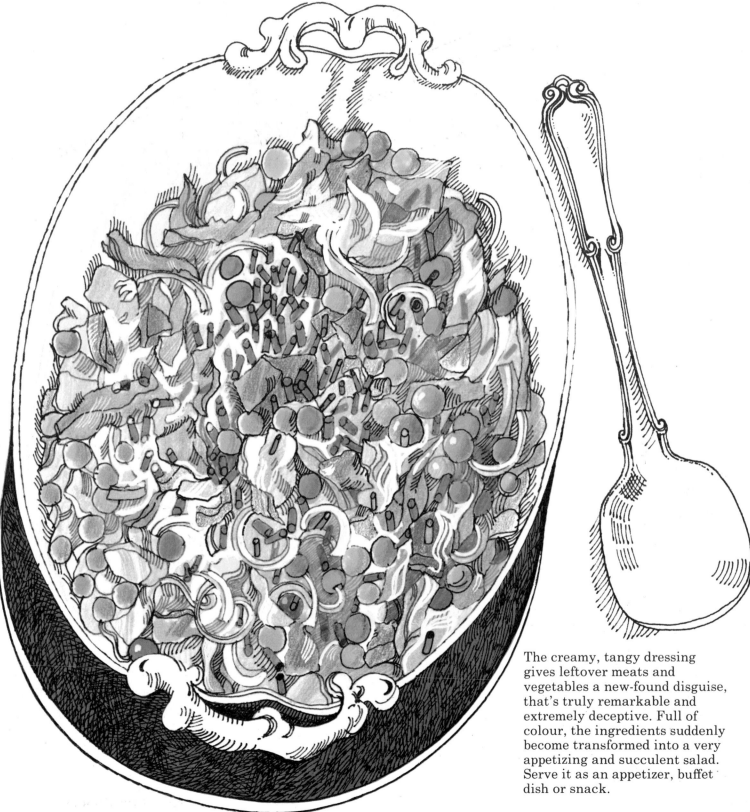

The creamy, tangy dressing gives leftover meats and vegetables a new-found disguise, that's truly remarkable and extremely deceptive. Full of colour, the ingredients suddenly become transformed into a very appetizing and succulent salad. Serve it as an appetizer, buffet dish or snack.

2 bunches watercress
½ cucumber, peeled and thinly sliced
100 g (4 oz) blue cheese, crumbled (optional)
3 tablespoons fresh lemon juice
8 tablespoons oil
salt and pepper to taste

(Serves 4)

1 Place the washed, trimmed and dried watercress in a salad bowl, add the sliced cucumber and the crumbled cheese (if used).

2 Toss it all together.

3 Into a screwtop jar put the lemon juice, oil, salt and pepper and shake it well until thoroughly mixed and thick and creamy.

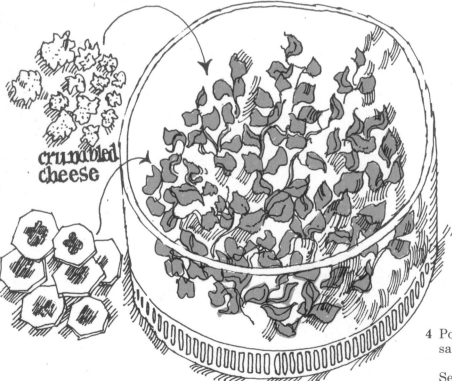

crumbled cheese

4 Pour this mixture over the salad, toss again gently.

Serve immediately!

Watercress Salad

This could be called a real English salad, in so far as watercress must be more readily available in England than anywhere else. The tangy lemon dressing gives this salad a smooth and delicate taste. Ideal as an accompaniment to any main course.

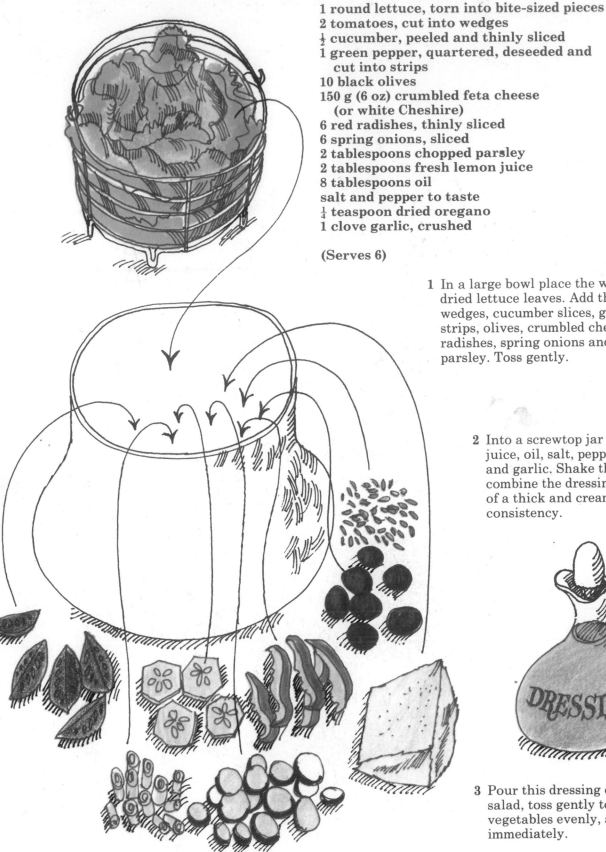

1 round lettuce, torn into bite-sized pieces
2 tomatoes, cut into wedges
½ cucumber, peeled and thinly sliced
1 green pepper, quartered, deseeded and
   cut into strips
10 black olives
150 g (6 oz) crumbled feta cheese
   (or white Cheshire)
6 red radishes, thinly sliced
6 spring onions, sliced
2 tablespoons chopped parsley
2 tablespoons fresh lemon juice
8 tablespoons oil
salt and pepper to taste
¼ teaspoon dried oregano
1 clove garlic, crushed

(Serves 6)

1 In a large bowl place the washed and dried lettuce leaves. Add the tomato wedges, cucumber slices, green pepper strips, olives, crumbled cheese, radishes, spring onions and the parsley. Toss gently.

2 Into a screwtop jar put the lemon juice, oil, salt, pepper, oregano and garlic. Shake the jar to combine the dressing, until it is of a thick and creamy consistency.

3 Pour this dressing over the salad, toss gently to coat all the vegetables evenly, and serve immediately.

GREEK SALAD

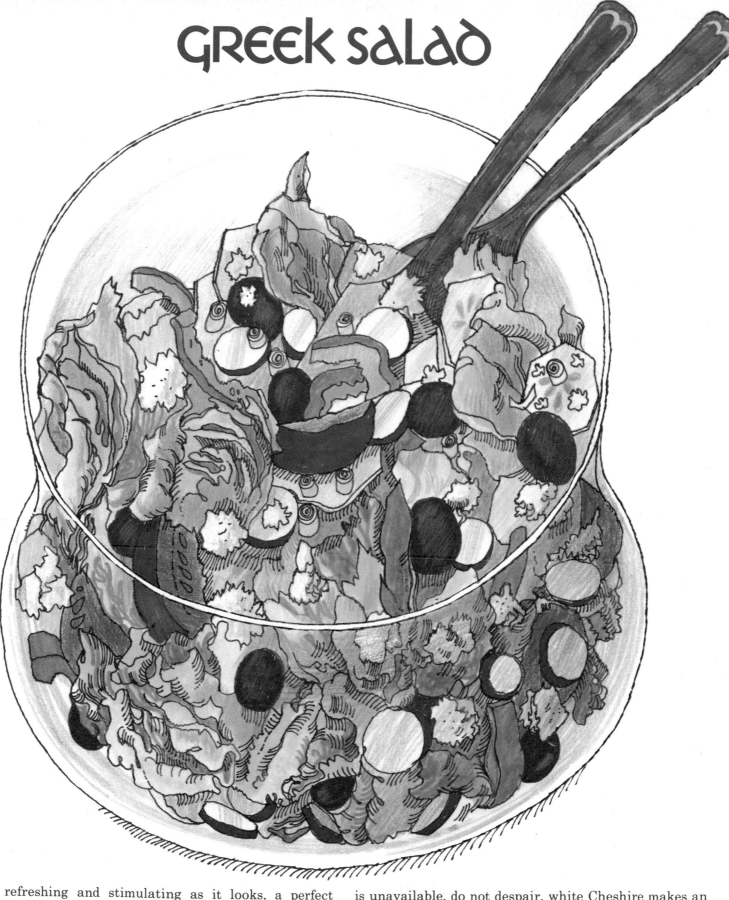

As refreshing and stimulating as it looks, a perfect blend of vegetables and cheese. The lemon dressing gives it a good tangy taste, while the feta cheese provides an authentic Mediterranean flavour. However, if feta cheese is unavailable, do not despair, white Cheshire makes an adequate substitute.

Excellent as a first course or as a side dish. A favourite in our household.

200 g (8 oz) thick sliced bacon
oil for frying bacon
6 heads chicory
2 hard-boiled eggs, chopped
100 ml (4 fl oz) oil
25 ml (1 fl oz) vinegar
salt and pepper to taste
2 tablespoons chopped parsley

(Serves 4–6)

1 Cut the bacon into small strips, put these into a saucepan of boiling water and boil
   them for 10 minutes to reduce the saltiness. Remove them with a draining spoon
   and dry on a paper towel. When thoroughly dry, fry the strips in the oil in a frying
   pan until crisp.

chopped
egg

2 Cut the chicory into
   13 mm (½-inch) thick
   slices and place them
   in a salad bowl. Add
   the chopped egg.

3 Make up the dressing
   by mixing together
   the oil, vinegar, salt
   and pepper. Pour this
   mixture over the salad
   and toss it together
   gently but thoroughly.

4 Place it on a nice platter
   and sprinkle the bacon bits
   and parsley on top.

   Serve very soon.

Flemish
Chicory Salad

A beautifully tangy flavour. Crisp and very
refreshing. An ideal combination of chicory, egg and bacon.
This salad goes well with any fried meats, chicken or fish.

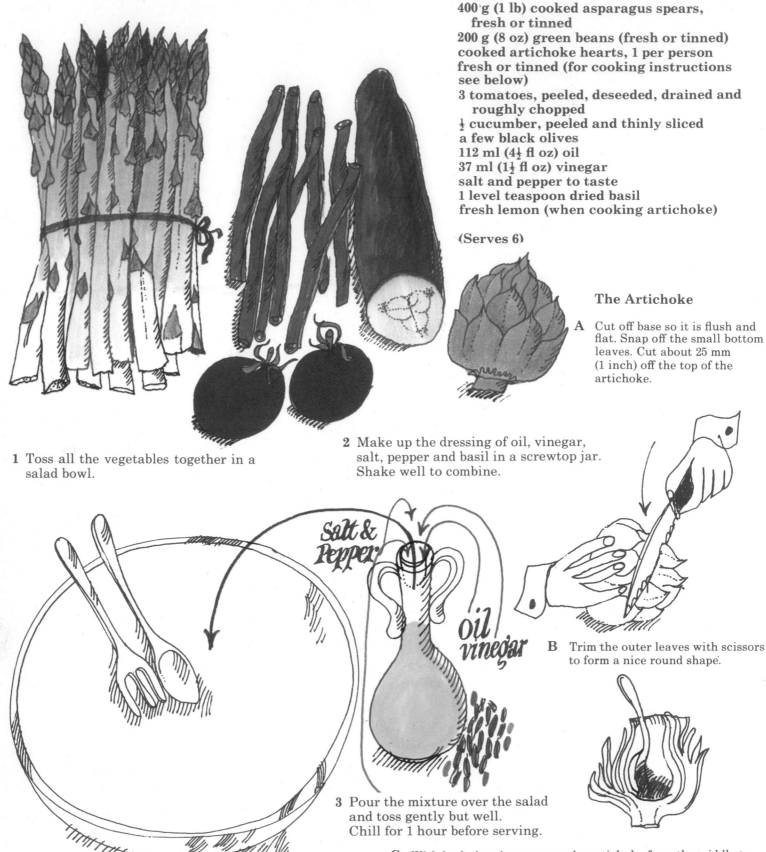

400 g (1 lb) cooked asparagus spears, fresh or tinned
200 g (8 oz) green beans (fresh or tinned)
cooked artichoke hearts, 1 per person fresh or tinned (for cooking instructions see below)
3 tomatoes, peeled, deseeded, drained and roughly chopped
½ cucumber, peeled and thinly sliced
a few black olives
112 ml (4½ fl oz) oil
37 ml (1½ fl oz) vinegar
salt and pepper to taste
1 level teaspoon dried basil
fresh lemon (when cooking artichoke)

(Serves 6)

The Artichoke

A Cut off base so it is flush and flat. Snap off the small bottom leaves. Cut about 25 mm (1 inch) off the top of the artichoke.

1 Toss all the vegetables together in a salad bowl.

2 Make up the dressing of oil, vinegar, salt, pepper and basil in a screwtop jar. Shake well to combine.

B Trim the outer leaves with scissors to form a nice round shape.

3 Pour the mixture over the salad and toss gently but well. Chill for 1 hour before serving.

C With both thumbs pry open the artichoke from the middle to expose the choke inside. Use a teaspoon to scrape out *all* of the hairy choke, and push the artichoke back into shape. Brush with lemon juice to prevent it discolouring and boil in salted water for 15 minutes. Drain and leave to cool before using.

4 Toss again lightly, decorate with olives and serve from the salad bowl or transfer it to a platter.

Italian Summer Salad

A real Italian salad – a typically Mediterranean combination. This is truly a magnificent recipe, grand enough to stand as an elegant starter, or it can make an unusual side dish to the main course.

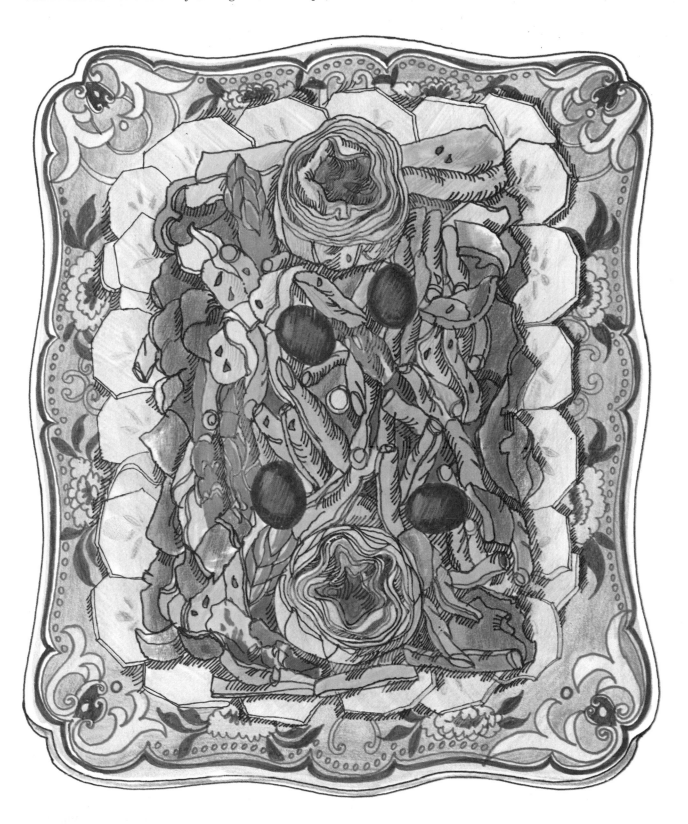

1 tin salmon
2 heaped tablespoons very finely
   chopped celery
2 hard-boiled eggs, chopped
4 tablespoons good mayonnaise
½ teaspoon curry powder

2 avocados
juice of 1 lemon
some nice lettuce leaves
paprika for garnish

(Serves 4)

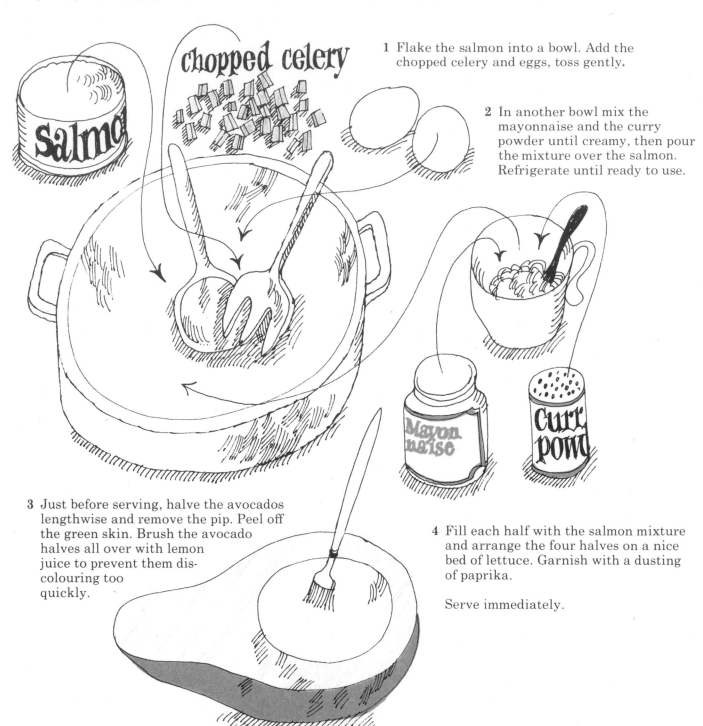

1 Flake the salmon into a bowl. Add the chopped celery and eggs, toss gently.

2 In another bowl mix the mayonnaise and the curry powder until creamy, then pour the mixture over the salmon. Refrigerate until ready to use.

3 Just before serving, halve the avocados lengthwise and remove the pip. Peel off the green skin. Brush the avocado halves all over with lemon juice to prevent them discolouring too quickly.

4 Fill each half with the salmon mixture and arrange the four halves on a nice bed of lettuce. Garnish with a dusting of paprika.

Serve immediately.

Salmon & Avocado Salad

This makes an excellent hors d'oeuvre winter and summer alike.
The smooth taste of the avocado blends ideally with the texture of
the salmon, eggs and celery. Very attractive to the eye, it can
grace any table with distinction.

1 small cucumber
125 ml (5 fl oz) oil
62 ml (2½ fl oz) white wine vinegar
1 clove garlic, crushed
1 teaspoon dried basil
salt and pepper to taste
200 g (8 oz) button mushrooms
5 spring onions, chopped
2 tablespoons chopped parsley
1 green pepper, quartered, deseeded and
   cut into strips
3 tomatoes, cut into wedges

(Serves 4)

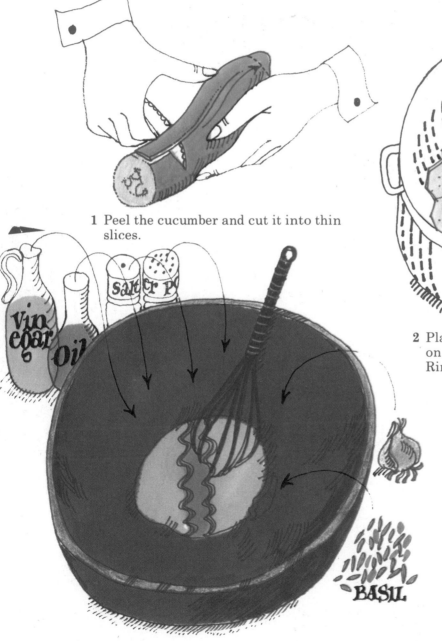

1 Peel the cucumber and cut it into thin slices.

2 Place them in a colander, sprinkle some salt on top and leave to drain for 30 minutes. Rinse them with cold water and dry thoroughly.

3 In a large bowl make the dressing by combining the oil, vinegar, garlic, basil, salt and pepper thoroughly.

4 Add the whole mushrooms and chopped spring onions, the drained cucumber slices and parsley. Toss it all together gently. Chill in the refrigerator for an hour or more.

5 Place the tomato wedges over the salad in the bowl and over them the green pepper strips. Toss all the vegetables gently but thoroughly.

Serve immediately.

MEXICAN GAZPACHO SALAD

A super salad when served really fresh and slightly chilled. Juicy and refreshing. An ideal side dish to accompany any meat course. A very attractive salad to show off to your friends.

1 lettuce head
6 red radishes, cut into slices
2 tomatoes, cut into slices
2 celery stalks, chopped
½ cucumber, peeled and diced
6 stuffed green olives, sliced
1 bunch watercress, trimmed
200 g (8 oz) cooked shrimp
    (fresh or frozen)
8 tablespoons oil

4 tablespoons vinegar
salt and pepper to taste
1 teaspoon dried tarragon
1 green pepper, cut into rings and deseeded

(Serves 4–6)

1 Wash and dry the lettuce leaves and tear them into
   bite-sized pieces. Place them in a salad bowl.

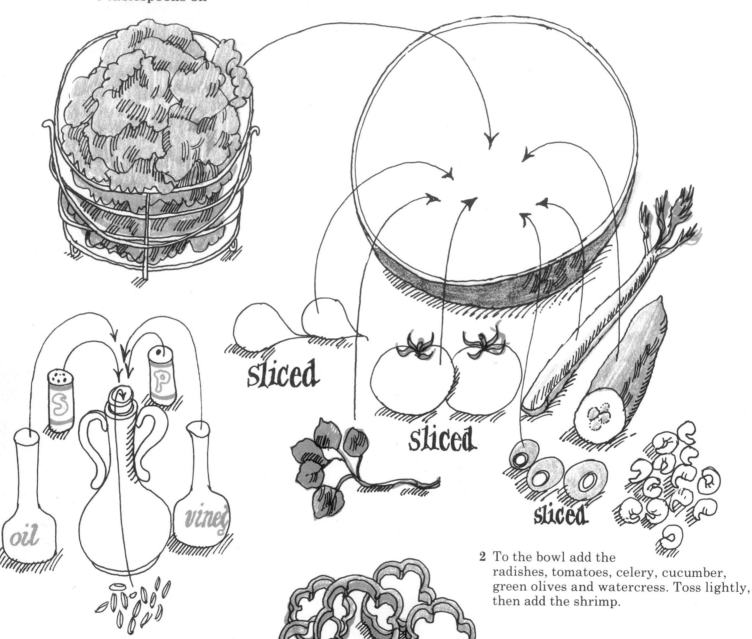

sliced

sliced

sliced

3 Combine oil, vinegar, salt, pepper
and tarragon in a screwtop jar and
shake well to combine. Pour it over
the salad and toss well.

2 To the bowl add the
radishes, tomatoes, celery, cucumber,
green olives and watercress. Toss lightly,
then add the shrimp.

4 Garnish the tossed salad with
   the green pepper rings.

   Serve immediately.

shrimp salad

An absolutely delicious salad, a beautiful
starter to a summer dinner party. Serve it as a
first course on small plates, with a garnish of
crisp toast, or brown bread and butter.

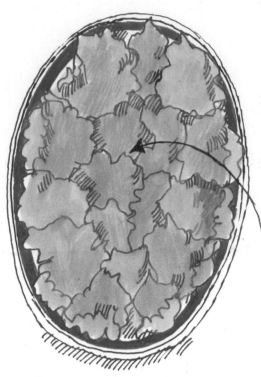

1 lettuce head
1 tin crabmeat or frozen crabmeat
   (as many servings as you will need)
6 heaped tablespoons good mayonnaise
4 tablespoons double cream
1 level desertspoon paprika
1 teaspoon Worcester sauce
5 spring onions, chopped
2 tablespoons fresh lemon juice
salt and pepper to taste
2 hard-boiled eggs, cut into wedges
lemon wedges
1 tablespoon chopped parsley

(Serves 2 for lunch and 4 as an hors d'oeuvre)

crabmeat

2 Place the crabmeat in the centre of the platter and pour over it this famous Louis dressing:

1 Arrange some nice large lettuce leaves on an attractive platter. Scatter the smaller leaves over them, or tear them into bite-sized pieces.

3 In a small bowl gently mix the mayonnaise, cream, paprika, Worcester sauce, spring onions, lemon juice, salt and pepper until well blended.

4 Garnish with wedges of hard-boiled egg and lemon and sprinkle with parsley.

Serve immediately.

CRAB SALAD LOUIS

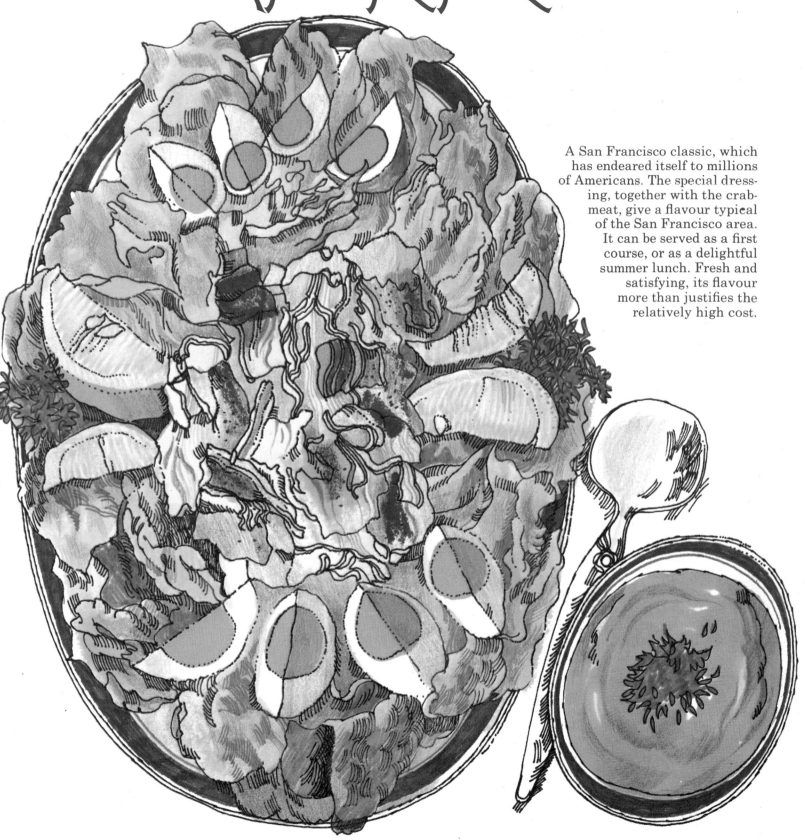

A San Francisco classic, which has endeared itself to millions of Americans. The special dressing, together with the crabmeat, give a flavour typical of the San Francisco area. It can be served as a first course, or as a delightful summer lunch. Fresh and satisfying, its flavour more than justifies the relatively high cost.

SALAD DRESSINGS

Mayonnaise

1 egg yolk
¼ teaspoon dry mustard
salt and pepper to taste
pinch of sugar
2 tablespoons wine vinegar
125 ml (¼ pint) oil

Place the egg yolk, mustard, salt, pepper and sugar in a deep bowl. Mix until well combined. Add the vinegar and whisk it with a wooden spoon or wire whisk until white and frothy. Add the oil, slowly drop by drop, whisking constantly, until the oil is used.
Occasionally the mayonnaise will curdle. Start again in another bowl with just one egg yolk. Whisk it constantly and slowly and add the curdled mayonnaise to it, by the teaspoonful, until it is all smooth and creamy. If the mayonnaise seems too thick for your needs, thin it down with a little cream.
Mayonnaise can also be made in a mixer, just follow the directions in your mixer book. However, mayonnaise made in a mixer does not have the same shine and texture.

Green Goddess Dressing

1 quantity of mayonnaise as above
3 chopped anchovy fillets
3 spring onions, chopped
2 tablespoons chopped parsley
1 teaspoon dried tarragon
1 heaped tablespoon chopped chives
2 tablespoons wine vinegar

Mix all the ingredients until smooth and creamy. Refrigerate before using on any green salad.

Thousand Island Dressing

1 quantity of mayonnaise as above
62 ml (2½ fl oz) ketchup
8 stuffed olives, finely chopped
1 small green pepper, finely chopped
1 tablespoon finely chopped chives or onion
1 hard-boiled egg, chopped
1 tablespoon chopped parsley

Mix all the ingredients together until smooth and creamy. Refrigerate before using on any green salad.

Yogurt Dressing

1 carton yogurt
1 small clove garlic, crushed
½ teaspoon dried oregano
1 tablespoon oil
salt and pepper to taste
1 fresh lemon (juice only)

Mix well, until smooth, the yogurt, crushed garlic, oregano, oil, salt and pepper. Then stir in the lemon juice and blend until smooth and creamy (about 280 calories).

Creamy French Dressing

1 tablespoon paprika
1 teaspoon sugar
1 teaspoon salt
75 ml (3 fl oz) vinegar
1 raw egg
225 ml (9 fl oz) oil

Combine paprika, sugar and salt. Add the vinegar and the egg and beat well. Add the oil in a slow stream, beating all the time, until the mixture is thick and creamy. Chill before serving over any green salad.

Blue Cheese Dressing

1 clove garlic
100 g (4 oz) blue cheese
2 teaspoons Worcester sauce
juice of 1 lemon
½ teaspoon dry mustard
¼ teaspoon paprika
1 tablespoon oil
salt and pepper to taste
1 quantity of mayonnaise as above

Mash garlic and cheese in a bowl. Add the Worcester sauce, lemon juice, mustard, paprika, oil, salt and pepper. Blend well. Add the mayonnaise and stir until smooth and creamy. Refrigerate before using over any green salad.

Watercress Dressing

2 tablespoons fresh lemon juice
1 tablespoon wine vinegar
½ teaspoon dried tarragon
125 ml (5 fl oz) oil
salt and pepper to taste
1 bunch watercress

Mix lemon juice, vinegar, tarragon, oil, salt and pepper until well blended. Then stir in the bunch of watercress, finely chopped. Use over any green salad.

Low Calorie Dressing

200 g (8 oz) cottage cheese
125 ml (5 fl oz) milk
salt and pepper to taste
2 tablespoons fresh lemon juice
1 small green pepper, chopped
5 spring onions, chopped
1 clove garlic, crushed

You can best do this in a mixer. Just swirl all the ingredients around until well blended. Refrigerate before using on any green salad.
If a mixer is not available, force the cottage cheese through a fine sieve and add all the other ingredients to it. Blend until smooth (about 350 calories).